YOU ARE
MY SUN,
MY MOON
AND STARS

YOU ARE MY SUN, MY MOON AND STARS

Compiled by Maria Medeiros

An Hachette UK Company
www.hachette.co.uk

Summersdale Publishers Ltd
Part of Octopus Publishing Group Limited
Carmelite House
50 Victoria Embankment
LONDON
EC4Y 0DZ
UK

www.summersdale.com

Printed and bound in China

ISBN: 978-1-80007-418-7

Substantial discounts on bulk quantities of Summersdale books are available to corporations, professional associations and other organizations. For details contact general enquiries: telephone: +44 (0) 1243 771107 or email: enquiries@summersdale.com.

TO..

FROM...

YOU ARE MY SUN,
MY MOON,
AND ALL MY
STARS.

E. E. CUMMINGS

LOVE IS SOMETHING THAT NEVER GOES OUT OF STYLE.

BEYONCÉ

I LOVE YOU
TO THE MOON
AND BACK

TO LOVE
SOMEONE IS
TO SEE A MIRACLE
INVISIBLE
TO OTHERS.

FRANÇOIS MAURIAC

LOVE IS

A GREAT BEAUTIFIER.

LOUISA MAY ALCOTT

The subject tonight is love and for tomorrow night as well.

HAFIZ

All love stories
are special,
but ours is
my favourite

IF I LOVED YOU LESS, I MIGHT BE ABLE TO TALK ABOUT IT MORE.

JANE AUSTEN

YOU ALWAYS
GAIN BY
GIVING LOVE.

REESE WITHERSPOON

You are
my today
and all of
my tomorrows

BEING DEEPLY LOVED
BY SOMEONE GIVES YOU

strength,

WHILE LOVING SOMEONE
DEEPLY GIVES YOU

courage.

LAO TZU

WHAT IS LOVE? IT IS THE MORNING AND THE EVENING STAR.

SINCLAIR LEWIS

It's amazing how the universe brings love to you.

Our love has no expiry date

WHAT IS DONE
IN LOVE
IS DONE WELL.

VINCENT VAN GOGH

I LOVE YOU – I AM
AT REST WITH YOU –
I HAVE COME HOME.

DOROTHY L. SAYERS

I LOVE
YOU FOR ALL
THAT YOU ARE
AND ALL THAT
YOU WILL BE

IN LOVE THE PARADOX OCCURS THAT TWO BEINGS BECOME ONE AND YET REMAIN TWO.

ERICH FROMM

LOVE IS THE WHOLE THING.

WE ARE
ONLY PIECES.

RUMI

If you remember me,
then I don't care if
everyone else forgets.

HARUKI MURAKAMI

Loving you was
never an option
— it was written
in the stars

IF I HAD TO
CHOOSE BETWEEN
BREATHING AND
LOVING YOU,
I WOULD USE
MY LAST BREATH
TO TELL YOU
I LOVE YOU.

ANONYMOUS

ONLY ONCE IN YOUR LIFE,
I TRULY BELIEVE, YOU
FIND SOMEONE WHO
CAN COMPLETELY TURN
YOUR WORLD AROUND.

BOB MARLEY

Out of all the people in the world, you are my one perfect person

Love
IS THE ONE
wild
CARD.

TAYLOR SWIFT

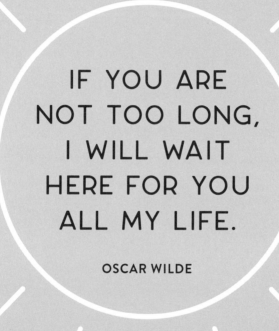

IF YOU ARE
NOT TOO LONG,
I WILL WAIT
HERE FOR YOU
ALL MY LIFE.

OSCAR WILDE

It's all about love.
We're either in love,
dreaming about
love, recovering from
it, wishing for it or
reflecting on it.

MICHAEL BUBLÉ

Love is looking
in the same
direction and
embracing
what life
offers together

THE GIVING
OF LOVE IS AN
EDUCATION
IN ITSELF.

ELEANOR ROOSEVELT

LOVE IS PROBABLY THE STRONGEST EMOTION THAT YOU CAN FEEL.

SHAWN MENDES

YOU ARE
ALWAYS THE
FIRST AND
LAST THING
ON MY MIND

I BELIEVE
THAT LOVE
COMES IN
ALL DIFFERENT
SHAPES, SIZES
AND COLOURS.

DEMI LOVATO

LOVE IS A TWO-WAY STREET

CONSTANTLY UNDER CONSTRUCTION.

CARROLL BRYANT

It sounds obvious, but I think you only learn to love again when you fall in love again.

ADELE

When I look
into your eyes,
galaxies collide

I CANNOT SAY
WHAT LOVES HAVE
COME AND GONE,
I ONLY KNOW
THAT SUMMER
SANG IN ME.

EDNA ST VINCENT MILLAY

CERTAIN THINGS IN
LIFE SIMPLY HAVE TO
BE EXPERIENCED AND
NEVER EXPLAINED. LOVE
IS SUCH A THING.

PAULO COELHO

I'm in love
with all the
little things
that make
you you

BLESSED IS THE

influence

OF ONE TRUE,

LOVING HUMAN

soul

ON ANOTHER.

GEORGE ELIOT

IF IT'S MEANT FOR ME, IT WILL BE.

JENNIFER HUDSON

You cannot touch love – but you feel the sweetness that it pours into everything.

HELEN KELLER

Your love was handmade just for me

LOVE
ISN'T SUPPOSED
TO MAKE SENSE.
IT'S COMPLETELY
ILLOGICAL.

JENNIFER E. SMITH

WE ARE MOST ALIVE WHEN WE'RE IN LOVE.

JOHN UPDIKE

LOVE IS HARD
TO FIND, HARD
TO HOLD ON
TO AND HARD
TO FORGET

LOVE DOESN'T
MAKE THE WORLD
GO ROUND.
LOVE IS WHAT
MAKES THE RIDE
WORTHWHILE.

FRANKLIN P. JONES

IF YOUR LOVE WERE A GRAIN OF SAND,

MINE WOULD BE A UNIVERSE OF BEACHES.

WILLIAM GOLDMAN

You are my heart,
my life, my one and
only thought.

ARTHUR CONAN DOYLE

Attraction
is temporary
but love is
permanent

A LOVING HEART IS THE BEGINNING OF ALL KNOWLEDGE.

THOMAS CARLYLE

MY HEART IS EVER
AT YOUR SERVICE.

WILLIAM SHAKESPEARE

You can hold
my hand for
a moment but
you have my
heart forever

IN LOVE THERE
ARE TWO THINGS —
bodies
AND
words.

JOYCE CAROL OATES

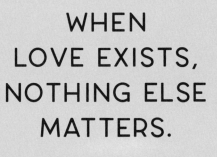

WHEN
LOVE EXISTS,
NOTHING ELSE
MATTERS.

ISABEL ALLENDE

To be brave is to love
someone unconditionally,
without expecting
anything in return.

MADONNA

The whole
universe
conspired in
helping me
find you

I'M VERY

COMFORTABLE

WITH WHO
I AM AND I LOVE
WHO I LOVE.

JESSIE J

IT'S GOOD TO BE LOVED. IT'S PROFOUND TO BE UNDERSTOOD.

PORTIA DE ROSSI

TRUE LOVE
DOESN'T
MEAN BEING
INSEPARABLE;
IT IS BEING
SEPARATED
AND NOTHING
CHANGES

IT'S EASY TO FALL IN LOVE. THE HARD PART IS FINDING SOMEONE TO CATCH YOU.

BERTRAND RUSSELL

LOVE IS EVER EVOLVING AND IT TAKES

COMPROMISE, WORK AND PATIENCE.

JESSICA ALBA

Remember, you have the capacity to choose. Choose life! Choose love!

JOSEPH MURRAY

We fall in love
by chance —
we stay in love
by choice

I WILL LOVE YOU TRULY FOREVER AND A DAY!

WILLIAM ROSE BENÉT

LOVE IS AN IRRESISTIBLE DESIRE TO BE IRRESISTIBLY DESIRED.

ROBERT FROST

You are
my favourite
notification

I FALL IN

love

WITH SOMEONE

BECAUSE OF THEIR

flaws.

CARA DELEVINGNE

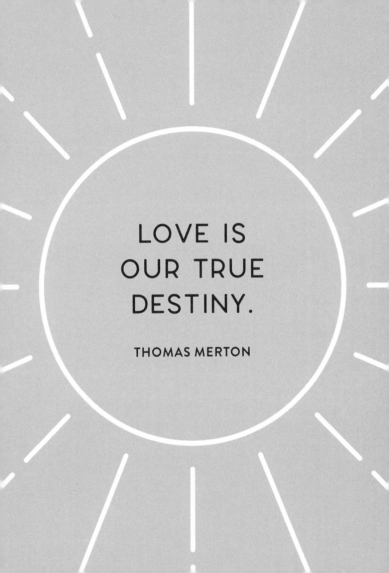

LOVE IS
OUR TRUE
DESTINY.

THOMAS MERTON

Love is space
and time measured
by the heart.

MARCEL PROUST

Loving you
is my biggest
weakness and
greatest strength

COME LIVE
IN MY
HEART,
AND PAY
NO RENT.

SAMUEL LOVER

DO NOT SEEK
THE BECAUSE —
IN LOVE THERE
IS NO BECAUSE,
NO EXPLANATION,
NO SOLUTIONS.

ANAÏS NIN

TO LOVE
IS NOTHING.
TO BE LOVED
IS SOMETHING.
BUT TO BE LOVED
BY THE PERSON
YOU LOVE IS
EVERYTHING.

LOVE IS LIKE A FRIENDSHIP CAUGHT ON FIRE.

BRUCE LEE

LIFE IS THE FLOWER FOR WHICH

LOVE IS THE HONEY.

VICTOR HUGO

If you've got
nothing else,
passion will get
you through.

HENRY CAVILL

You're not my
number one —
you're my
only one

LOVE IS THAT
CONDITION IN
WHICH THE
HAPPINESS OF
ANOTHER PERSON
IS ESSENTIAL TO
YOUR OWN.

ROBERT A. HEINLEIN

IF GRASS CAN
GROW THROUGH
CEMENT, LOVE CAN
FIND YOU AT EVERY
TIME IN YOUR LIFE.

CHER

When I
met you,
the stars
aligned

THE DEED OF

love

IS STRONGER

THAN

words.

PEARL BAILEY

LOVE
IS NEVER
WRONG.

MELISSA ETHERIDGE

Speak low if you speak love.

WILLIAM SHAKESPEARE

Our love is a journey starting at forever and finishing at never

IN ALL THE
WORLD, THERE
IS NO HEART
FOR ME LIKE
YOURS.

MAYA ANGELOU

DON'T CHOOSE THE ONE WHO IS BEAUTIFUL TO THE WORLD. BUT RATHER, CHOOSE THE ONE WHO MAKES YOUR WORLD BEAUTIFUL.

HARRY STYLES

YOU ARE
MY PAST,
PRESENT AND
FUTURE

BUT THAT'S WHAT LOVE IS: TO GIVE EVERYTHING, TO SACRIFICE EVERYTHING, WITHOUT EXPECTING ANYTHING IN RETURN.

ALBERT CAMUS

LOVE IS SOMETHING SENT FROM HEAVEN

TO WORRY THE HELL OUT OF YOU.

DOLLY PARTON

There is no
remedy for love
but to love more.

HENRY DAVID THOREAU

I will love you
for as long as
the moon shines
its guiding light

TRUE LOVE
DOESN'T COME
TO YOU;
IT HAS TO BE
INSIDE YOU.

JULIA ROBERTS

TO LOVE AND BE LOVED
IS TO FEEL THE SUN
FROM BOTH SIDES.

DAVID VISCOTT

You are
what appeared
when I wished
upon a star

MY LOVE IS

selfish.

I CANNOT

breathe

WITHOUT YOU.

JOHN KEATS

LOVE
MAKES YOUR
SOUL CRAWL
OUT FROM ITS
HIDING PLACE.

ZORA NEALE HURSTON

When you're in love,
you're so happy
that you want to
tell people about it.

EMILY BLUNT

I want to love you twice in this lifetime — that's now and forever

THERE IS ONLY
ONE HAPPINESS
IN LIFE:
TO LOVE
AND BE LOVED.

GEORGE SAND

I BELIEVE
IN LOVE.

JENNIFER LOPEZ

YOU ARE MY
HEART'S BIGGEST
ADVENTURE

IF YOU FALL IN LOVE WITH THEIR EYES, YOU'LL BE IN LOVE FOREVER.

ED SHEERAN

LOVE IS THE GREATEST

REFRESHMENT IN LIFE.

PABLO PICASSO

Wherever
you are, and
whatever you do,
be in love.

RUMI

You are my
definition
of perfect

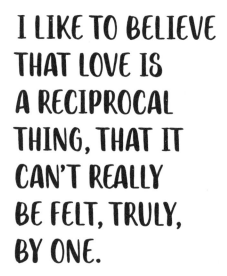

I LIKE TO BELIEVE
THAT LOVE IS
A RECIPROCAL
THING, THAT IT
CAN'T REALLY
BE FELT, TRULY,
BY ONE.

SEAN PENN

LOVE HAS NOTHING TO
DO WITH WHAT YOU ARE
EXPECTING TO GET —
ONLY WITH WHAT YOU
ARE EXPECTING TO GIVE.

KATHARINE HEPBURN

I love you
just the way
you are

WE
love
BECAUSE IT'S THE
ONLY TRUE
adventure.

NIKKI GIOVANNI

LOVE IS
A FRIENDSHIP
SET TO MUSIC.

JOSEPH CAMPBELL

Love isn't something you find. Love is something that finds you.

LORETTA YOUNG

Our
love story
will never
cease

I THINK THE
PERFECTION
OF LOVE IS THAT
IT'S NOT PERFECT.

TAYLOR SWIFT

THE ONLY THING
WE NEVER GET
ENOUGH OF IS LOVE;
AND THE ONLY THING
WE NEVER GIVE
ENOUGH OF IS LOVE.

HENRY MILLER

YOU ARE MY
GUIDING STAR IN
THE NIGHT SKY

LOVE IS A BEAUTIFUL DREAM.

WILLIAM SHARP

IT MAKES ME A LOT HAPPIER WHEN

I'M SHARING MY LIFE WITH SOMEBODY.

KYLIE JENNER

Love is just a word until someone comes along and gives it meaning.

PAULO COELHO

Our love is like
a roller coaster.
Every time I
reach the top,
I fall again
— for you

WHEN YOU'RE
LUCKY ENOUGH
TO MEET YOUR
ONE PERSON,
THEN LIFE TAKES
A TURN FOR
THE BEST.

JOHN KRASINSKI

LOVE NEVER CLAIMS, IT EVER GIVES.

MAHATMA GANDHI

Your love
completes me

WHERE
THERE IS GREAT

love

THERE ARE ALWAYS

miracles.

WILLA CATHER

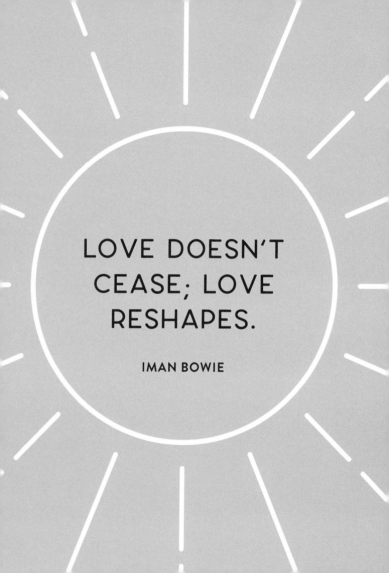

LOVE DOESN'T
CEASE; LOVE
RESHAPES.

IMAN BOWIE

A loving heart
is the truest wisdom.

CHARLES DICKENS

True love
is a bridge
across an
ocean

IF I LOVE YOU
THAT'LL ALWAYS
BE THE CASE,
EVEN IF IT'S FROM
THE DISTANCE.

ALEXANDRA ELLE

I LOVE YOU NOT ONLY
FOR WHAT YOU ARE,
BUT FOR WHAT I AM
WHEN I AM WITH YOU.

ELIZABETH BARRETT BROWNING

IN THIS WORLD
YOU ARE ONE
PERSON, BUT TO
ME, YOU ARE
THE WORLD

I SWEAR I
COULDN'T LOVE
YOU MORE THAN
I DO RIGHT NOW,
AND YET I KNOW
I WILL TOMORROW.

LEO CHRISTOPHER

LOVE IS A GAME THAT TWO

CAN PLAY AND BOTH WIN.

EVA GABOR

You know
you're in love when
you can't fall asleep
because reality is
finally better than
your dreams.

DR SEUSS

Our love grows
stronger every
day with
the universe
on our side

LOVE IS
THE BEST THING
IN THE WORLD,
AND THE THING
THAT LIVES
THE LONGEST.

HENRY VAN DYKE

IT'S ALWAYS WRONG TO
HATE, BUT IT'S NEVER
WRONG TO LOVE.

LADY GAGA

The most
rewarding thing
I have done in
my lifetime is
to fall in love
with you

EVERYTHING IS

clearer

WHEN YOU'RE IN

love.

JOHN LENNON

I WILL ALWAYS
BELIEVE IN LOVE.

KIM KARDASHIAN

I saw that you were perfect and I loved you. Then I saw that you were not perfect and I loved you even more.

ANGELITA LIM

You are the
brightest of
all the stars,
and you light
up my world

LOVE IS
DIVINE ONLY
AND DIFFICULT
ALWAYS.

TONI MORRISON

IF YOU TRULY LOVE
SOMETHING LET IT GO.
IF IT COMES BACK IT
WAS MEANT TO BE.

SELENA GOMEZ

THE MOMENT
I SAW YOU,
I KNEW

YOU DON'T REALLY GET TO CHOOSE WHO YOU FALL IN LOVE WITH. LOVE CHOOSES YOU.

BRAD PITT

TRUE LOVE IS RARE, AND IT'S THE ONLY THING THAT GIVES LIFE REAL MEANING.

NICHOLAS SPARKS

I closed my mouth and spoke to you in a hundred silent ways.

RUMI

You will forever
be my always

I FELL IN LOVE
THE WAY YOU FALL
ASLEEP: SLOWLY,
AND THEN ALL
AT ONCE.

JOHN GREEN

AMONG THE COUNTLESS PEOPLE IN THE WORLD, TWO WILL FIND EACH OTHER AGAINST ALL THE ODDS AND BEAT AS A SINGLE ETERNAL HEART.

JENNIFER LAWRENCE

I wish
I found you
sooner so I
could love
you longer

IF I HAD A

flower

FOR EVERY TIME
I THOUGHT OF YOU...
I COULD WALK
THROUGH MY GARDEN

forever.

ALFRED, LORD TENNYSON

THE BEST
THING TO HOLD
ON TO IN LIFE IS
EACH OTHER.

AUDREY HEPBURN

We come to love
not by finding
a perfect person,
but by learning
to see an imperfect
person perfectly.

SAM KEEN

If I know what love is, it is because of you.

HERMANN HESSE

WHERE THERE
IS LOVE,
THERE IS NO
QUESTION.

YOGI BHAJAN

JUST LIKE THE
MOON AND STARS
ONLY EVER NEED
THE SKY – I ONLY
EVER NEED YOU

If you're interested in finding
out more about our books, find us
on Facebook at Summersdale Publishers,
on Twitter at @Summersdale and on
Instagram at @summersdalebooks.

www.summersdale.com

Image credits

Sun and moon icon on cover and throughout
© LaInspiratriz/Shutterstock.com; stars and dots
pattern used on cover and throughout © sini4ka/
Shutterstock.com; moon phases icon used on p.11
and throughout © WinWin artlab/Shutterstock.
com; stars used on p.6 and throughout © Qilli/
Shutterstock.com; background texture on p.17 and
throughout © Jamie Farrant/Shutterstock.com